Social Skills for Kids

The Ultimate Guide to Developing Manners, Etiquette, and Positive Behavior to Promote Confidence and Make Friends

Table of Contents

Introduction

The art of socializing is learned through practice and exposure. It's a skill that can be acquired by anyone, anywhere. Improving your social skills will improve every part of your life, from how people perceive you to how you create new friendships and maintain old ones. The world is different now than it was just a few decades ago, and as a result, we have new challenges and opportunities to learn new social skills.

This exciting book is your guide to learning and honing your social skills. Inside, you'll find chapters on self-expression, basic manners, listening, and making friends. You'll learn how to initiate conversations and share your opinions. You'll learn about short and long-term goals and how to define the steps necessary to get from where you are now to where you want to be.

This book is written as a workbook, allowing you to go on your own adventure throughout the following pages. The activities are easy to understand and represent real-world approaches to social skills. The best part is you'll have a ton of fun learning them and won't even realize you're practicing them.

There is no limitation when it comes to what can be learned here because the possibilities are endless when it comes to social skills. You'll find that you are always learning; the more you learn, the better off you will be! Knowledge is power. Knowledge is confidence. Knowledge is respect. So, what are you waiting for? It's time to become a "social" genius!

Letter to Parents

Dear Parents,

Thank you for caring about your child and recognizing the importance of developing their social skills. While school and home are great places to learn, children learn through shared experiences and discussions with friends, teachers, and strangers. They learn by having fun, making friends, sharing, and showing gratitude. With practice and encouragement, any child, including yours, can master social skills.

As your child's first teacher, you should listen to their feelings, build their self-esteem, and offer constant encouragement. This book is designed to help reinforce the social skills you're already teaching your child. Children learn best when activities feel like play, so encourage them to try new things with patience and structure.

Children naturally gravitate towards social settings where they can learn and experience social skills. As their support system, help them choose appropriate settings and encourage appropriate behavior while having fun. This book can be read together or independently, and it will help your child recognize that everyone struggles with social skills at times. By taking it one day at a time, laying a few bricks every day, your child will build their social skills brick by brick.

Letter to Child Reader

Congratulations! You have just taken the first step on an exciting journey to becoming a more confident and socially skilled person! You are in charge of your own social development, which is a big deal. It means that if you want to learn how to talk to people, make friends, and get along with others, you have the power to do so. There are many different sides to socializing, and some can be difficult for you as a child, but don't worry, there are tons of tips here to help you become the best version of yourself and have lots of fun in the process.

You're growing fast, and in no time at all, you'll be a full-fledged adult member of society, ready to change the world around you. Or at least your own little corner of it. The age-old question is this: What kind of person do you want to be? The answer to that is completely up to you, and that is what makes childhood so magical and special: being able to do anything you put your mind to. You may find yourself lost in the wonder and excitement of being older and bigger than you are now, but there is much to be gained from the journey there – a journey that has already begun.

Within the pages of this fantastic book, you will learn all kinds of things about social interaction, communication, and behavior. Some of it may be challenging to grasp, while some may be easy, but take it one tip at a time, and before you know it, you'll be an expert. If you are unsure of anything, ask your parents or any other trusted adult for assistance. With some effort on your part, you will watch yourself grow and change in ways that will mark your childhood as a wonderful and special time. All you have to do is open the pages and begin.

Chapter 1: Please and Thank You: Basic Manners

"Please" and "Thank you" are two of the most basic manners anyone should know, yet it is surprising how many people forget to use them. Manners are essential, and having them can mean the difference between a nice day at school and a rotten one, a great day at the store, and a terrible one. When you know how to use basic manners, you'll be able to make friends and deal with many situations. You'll be able to get through school, parties, and public places much easier. Plus, you'll be less likely to get into trouble or get picked on.

Saying "Please" and "Thank you" will always make a difference with your friends and family.
https://unsplash.com/photos/j28h3uNmKCA

You may have already noticed that quite a few people in the world don't say these two words very often or at all. You may have even been on the receiving end of this behavior, or you may sometimes be a bit guilty. Either way, by learning to say please and thank you as often as needed, you can avoid many unnecessary issues and make yourself and the people around you much happier. Plus, saying please and thank you doesn't take any extra effort. It's not like being polite will hurt you. All it means is that you're kind and considerate, and that's a good thing!

Still, what's so great about learning to say please and thank you, you ask? How are those two phrases going to make your life better? Well, for starters, they will help you get what you want easier. Whether you're asking your brother to play with you or getting your parents to give you some money for lunch, saying please and thank you will make everything easier. You don't have to be embarrassed about asking for things anymore because saying please and thank you will let the person on the other end of the conversation feel good about helping you.

Also, saying please and thank you is much better than not. You want to be kind and courteous to everyone you meet, and saying please and thank you is one of the best ways to do that. In a world where people are often rude, impolite, impatient, and disrespectful, it's always nice to stand out from the crowd simply by being polite.

Finally, just because you say please and thank you doesn't mean you'll get what you want every single time. In fact, there will be some days when saying please and thank you isn't enough, which can leave you feeling a little frustrated. On those days, remember that being polite doesn't mean you'll always get what you want, but you have even fewer chances of getting anything from anyone if you don't have good manners.

Now that we've covered why saying please and thank you is so important, take a look at the practical side of things. How exactly do you say those two little phrases? Saying please is really easy. It's just one small word that you tack onto the beginning, or sometimes the end, of your request, depending on the situation. Say it out loud right now if you're having trouble remembering it. You can even try these simple sentences:

1. "Please give me a cookie," or "I'd really like a cookie, please."
2. "Please let me stay up a little longer," or "Could I please stay up a little longer?"
3. "Please turn down the music; it's too loud," or "I'd really like it if you turned the music down, please."

Now that you've learned how to say please, how do you say thank you? It's pretty much as easy as saying please. *Thank you* means gratitude. It means you recognize that someone has done something for you and are happy about it. There are a ton of ways to express this. Here are a few:

1. "Thank you so much for helping me move my things" or "I appreciate everything you did. Thank you."
2. "Thank you for the birthday card" or "I really like this card, thank you."
3. "Thank you for letting me borrow your bike," or "I had fun riding your bike, thank you."
4. Or just "Thank you."

You'll find that once you start saying these words every time you need to get something, ask for something, or are thankful for something, the thought of not saying them will seem weird and uncomfortable.

Say please
and thank you

Other Kinds of Good Manners

Please and thank you are important, but they're not the only basic manners everyone should have. There are many other ways to show respect and kindness to people. Good manners can also look like:

Listening without interrupting: When someone is talking to you, it's good manners to listen patiently and not interrupt. Let them finish speaking before you say what you want to say. It shows that you value their words and respect their right to be heard. For example, your friend is excitedly telling you about their new parrot. Now, instead of interrupting with your own story, patiently listen until they finish. Then, you can say what's on your mind and ask your questions about their bird.

Using kind words: Good manners include using kind and gentle words when talking to people. Instead of using hurtful or mean words, choose respectful words that make people feel good. Let's say your classmate worked hard on a drawing. Instead of looking for something wrong with it, you can say something like, "Wow, you put a lot of effort into this! I really like the colors you used." See?

Being inclusive: Good manners mean including everyone and making sure nobody feels left out. If you see someone sitting alone or feeling lonely, invite them to join you and your friends. Being inclusive shows that you care about people and want everyone to feel welcome.

Respecting personal space: Respecting personal space means giving others enough physical room to feel comfortable. Not everyone likes to be touched or hugged, so it's good manners to ask for permission before touching someone or entering their personal space. Imagine you want to give your friend a high-five, but they don't seem like they want to high-five you back. Instead of insisting, you can say, "Is it okay if we high-five? If not, that's totally fine, too."

Being patient: To be patient is to wait. Good manners include being patient, especially when waiting for your turn or when someone needs extra time to do something. Take a deep breath and remember that being patient shows respect and consideration for others and what they need. For example, you're waiting for your turn at the ice cream stand, and the person in front of you is taking a bit longer than you'd like. Instead of getting frustrated and saying something rude, you can take a deep breath and come up with a good reason for why they are taking so long. Maybe they're getting a lot of ice cream or having trouble deciding between flavors. Who knows?

Apologizing when you make a mistake: We all make mistakes sometimes, and it's good manners to take responsibility for them. If you accidentally hurt someone's feelings or do something wrong, saying "I'm sorry" shows that you care about the impact of what you did and want to make things right. Say you accidentally bump into someone in the hallway; you can say, "Oh, I'm sorry! I didn't mean to bump into you. Are you okay?" This shows that you acknowledge your mistake and are genuinely concerned about the other person. It also shows maturity and your willingness to learn from your mistakes.

Cleaning up after yourself: Cleaning up after yourself means taking responsibility for your own messes. If you play with your toys or have a snack, you need to put everything back where it belongs when you're done. This way, you keep things organized and show respect for shared spaces.

Exercises

There are plenty of things you can do to practice saying please and thank you, but here are a few exercises you can use right now and even try with your friends. This way, everyone will get the chance to practice!

A Manners Challenge: This is a fun challenge you can do with your family or friends. For the entire day, say *please* and *thank you* as much as possible. Make it fun by counting how many times you can say them, tallying up points for each one. When you come home at night, see who got the most points, then feel free to brag about it!

Role-Playing: For this exercise, you'll need the help of your friends or family. You'll need two people at least, but the more, the better. You all need to decide on a scenario that will challenge you to say please and thank you as much as possible. For example, one person will be the waiter or waitress, and the other people need to come in and politely order a meal, or someone pretends to be a storekeeper, and another person asks for a refund or exchange. Another good one is getting someone to ask for directions, and the other person politely responds. The point is to invent a situation that requires you to be polite and say please and thank you so that you'll be ready whenever needed.

Manners Bingo: This is a great game for children. You can make the bingo sheet, which is more fun, or print one off the internet. You'll need a large sheet of paper, a pencil, and some markers to make it yourself. Draw about eight or more squares on the sheet, depending on your paper size. You'll need one square for "thank you," one for "please," and maybe a couple for "thank you so much." You can add other polite sentences like "Excuse me," "I'm sorry," and "You're welcome." You can also draw little people or animals in the squares so that it looks more exciting. Whenever you say one of the sentences on your bingo sheet, give the box a large tick with a marker. When you finish the bingo sheet, you'll see that you've practiced the words in many different ways.

BINGO

PLEASE	THANK YOU	EXCUSE ME	I'M SORRY	LET'S PLAY
KNOCK KNOCK	HELLO	BE KIND	HOLD DOORS	CAN I HELP
NO MEAN NAMES	PLEASE PASS THE BUTTER	FREE	COVER YOUR MOUTH	WAIT PATIENTLY
SIT UP STRAIGHT	BE A GOOD SPORT	DO NOT SMACK	HELP CLEAN UP	YOU'RE WELCOME
ASK BEFORE TAKING	BE HONEST	I LIKE YOUR SHIRT	BE HELPFUL	RESPECT OTHERS

You're now much more prepared to be polite and use the right words when necessary. You've learned why it's necessary to be polite and how to do it, so when you find yourself thinking, "There's no need to say 'please' or 'thank you,'" think again!

Being polite can mean big things for your relationships and how others see you. It not only shows that you respect and consider others, but it also says good things about your character. By using polite words and phrases as often as possible, you'll notice that you enjoy having conversations with people more and that life is easier than it was beforehand. So don't underestimate the power of a simple "please" or "thank you." These tiny words can go a long way in building meaningful connections with people and leaving a lasting impression.

Chapter 2: Make Friends and Keep Them

Making friends can be hard, *even for adults*. At your age, you're still learning how society works and figuring out who you are. It takes a lot of effort and time to figure out who your "people" are, who is right for you, and who will accept you as you are. You may think the hardest part of forming a new friendship is making it through that awkward first conversation, but maintaining those friendships is an even bigger challenge.

Friendships are important, and there are many reasons for this, some of which you already know. Good friends make you happy when you are sad (or mad), they cheer you on when you're celebrating something big (or small), they share experiences with you that make you laugh, they understand who you are and who you want to be, and usually, you are into the same things.

Good friends can cheer you up if you're sad.

Good friends also help you be a good friend in return. They understand what you need and when you need it. They help you be kind and trustworthy, even when life is hard, and good friends make you feel special. They know what makes you happy and go out of their way to make it happen.

Are You a Good Friend?

Friendship is a two-way street. So, you need to be a good friend to others too. It's not enough to want to be their friend –you need to be a good friend who is kind, respectful, and trustworthy. So, how do you make the leap from where you are now to becoming a great friend? What builds solid friendships that never end in burning bridges or an ugly breakup? Here are some simple, easy-to-live-by friendship principles you can use:

Keep It Real

Real friends are loyal and honest. They have each other's backs. They don't spread rumors about each other or put each other down. They are there for each other when times get tough. They do stuff for one another without expecting anything in return.

Be a Good Friend By: Being loyal and honest. Don't put your friend down, even if it's to say, "I told you so." Stand up for your friend when the pressure is on. Ask them how they are doing and show up for them often, not just at special times.

Be Patient with Each Other's Changes and Mistakes

If you are a good friend to someone, you know they will make mistakes sometimes, even if it's the dumbest thing you've ever seen them do.

Be a Good Friend By: Being patient with your friend when they mess up. Even if you get mad, make sure you walk away or take time out to calm down before trying to converse with them. Take them aside and help them when needed, even if that means holding back on your opinion for a while.

Be Kind

Kindness is probably the easiest thing to remember, but do you ever think about it? Do you notice it in others? Would you say you're a kind person? Kindness is a gift. You have no idea how much someone's life can change when kindness enters the picture.

Always be kind.
https://unsplash.com/photos/COzpyQtcqMA

Be a Good Friend By: Being kind to others, especially your friends and family. Think about their feelings before you say or do something that may be hurtful or difficult for them to hear. Show your friends and family that you are a good friend by being kind every day.

Be Respectful

Respect is a huge part of being a good friend. Respect means treating others the way you'd like to be treated. If you have ever thought about who you respect most, it's probably people who are kind, good-hearted, and respectful.

Be a Good Friend By: Not saying mean things about others. Even if you think your friend deserves it, don't say mean things to hurt them or make them feel bad. This may lead to fights and broken hearts that can last a long time, even years.

Be Trustworthy

Trust is everything when it comes to friendships. It means believing that your friends will be there for you when you need them. It means knowing what your friend is or is not capable of doing. It also means believing your friend will be kind to you and treat you well, no matter what. Everyone likes to feel safe in their relationships, and when there is trust, there is safety.

Be a Good Friend By: Not breaking promises to your friends or backing out of commitments you make. If they are counting on you, be there for them.

Listen to Them

Being a good friend means listening to your friends, not only when they tell you to but also when you can feel that it is what they need. A good listener is always a better friend.

Be a Good Friend By: Listening to your friend without judgment or interruption. Let them finish speaking even if you don't understand what they're saying or why something is happening. Respect them, their feelings, and their ideas by giving them attention, even if it means being completely quiet.

Show Empathy

Being a good friend means you understand what your friends are going through. Empathy shows that you care and that you can be a comfort to others when they need it. It is understanding what others are feeling or experiencing. It's about putting yourself in their shoes and seeing things from their point of view.

Be a Good Friend By: Being willing to listen and respond when your friends need support, advice, help, or want someone to be there for them. Be aware of the things going on in their lives and be there for them when needed.

Give Back

Do things for your friends without expecting anything in return. It's about taking risks and helping your friends grow. Give back and spread love to each other, even if all you do is say something kind, hold a door open, or lend them your favorite book. All these things show you care.

Be a Good Friend By: Volunteering your time to help or make a difference in your friend's life. This will make them feel included and appreciated, ensuring a beautiful, long-lasting friendship.

Exercises

This is the fun part! Keep reading to find three games that you can play to help you make and maintain good friendships. You will understand more about what you value in a friend and what it takes to be a good friend.

1. **Friendship Role-Play:** For this game, you and your friends or family will get together and act out a few plays that involve friendship. Come up with a few different scenes, including fights (fake fights, of course), fun times, and even hard choices. Each person will have a role to play that is either a good friend or a bad friend, and after you're done, you all can talk about each scene and how you all felt about the part that you each played.

2. **Friendship Circle:** This game is a simple one. It's where you get a group of friends together and create your own private circle. If you don't know as much as you want about who is in your circle, this game will help you figure it out. First, all the players sit in a circle on the grass or floor with their legs crossed. Every person thinks of something they can share with the group, including what they like about other group members, favorite things to do together, or even something bothering them. After everyone shares their thoughts, you will learn a lot about your friends and how you can be a better friend to them.

3. **Friendship Journal:** If you already enjoy writing or have a diary, this game is right up your alley. A friendship journal is a secret book you can use to write about your friendships and how you feel about them. It's a good way to get things off your chest and think about what you like and don't like in a friend. You don't have to write down only what being a good friend is. You can also put down ideas for improving your relationships with friends, like meeting up more, having sleepovers, or going to summer school together. You can also write lessons you have learned from your friendships in the past and how you think you could use those lessons now.

Journal

_____

_____

_____

_____

_____

_____

_____

_____

_____

_____

_____

_____

_____

_____

_____

_____

Journal

_____

_____

_____

_____

_____

_____

_____

_____

_____

_____

_____

_____

_____

_____

_____

_____

_____

Friendships Journal

Friendships status:

Describe yourself:

Draw yourself:

My hobbies are:

I hate ...

My best friend is:

My favorite season is:

My favorite flower is

My favorite color is:

The holiday I like best is:

The country I wold like to see:

The movie that I'd like to see again is ...

Describe your best moments ...

Tips for Making Friends

- Put yourself out there. Don't be shy. Make eye contact if someone gets your attention, but don't stare for too long, as it might make you look like a creeper.

- Don't be afraid to smile. If someone does smile back, that's your golden opportunity to make conversation.

- Be yourself. Don't put on a show or be someone you're not for the sake of being liked. Being genuine goes a long way.

- Be friendly and approachable. People are less likely to want to get to know you if you act cold and distant.

- Sign up for activities that you enjoy. Who knows? Maybe you'll meet some new friends there!

- If someone new comes into your life, try your best to get along with them.

- Know what you're interested in. Some people are more outgoing, and others are more quiet. No one is better than the other. We're all different, and that's a good thing.

- If you want to get to know a new person, try starting with a question that's not too personal or hard to answer. Like, "What school do you go to?" Or "How long have you lived here?"

- Finally, always remember to be kind and respect everyone you meet. It will make other people want to be your friends, too.

You can be friends with anyone by being kind and respectful.
https://www.pexels.com/photo/little-girls-and-boys-having-fun-playing-with-colorful-balls-8613146/

Not every friendship will last forever. In fact, many don't, which is totally normal –even for really good friends –but if you focus on being a good friend, you are bound to make great, long-lasting friendships. You see, you don't need a lot of friends; you only need a few good ones. Remember this because you'll understand it better when you're older.

Chapter 3: How to Be Super Kind

Kindness is a word that doesn't sound as exciting as superheroes or princesses. Yet, being kind is one of the biggest superhero moves you could ever pull off! This chapter will show you how to be a superhero every day by paying it forward with kindness (no capes or tights required).

Being kind is a superpower that helps your friends.
https://unsplash.com/photos/dDrQPSbYQRk

When you hear the word kind, what comes to mind? Maybe you're imagining a sweet old lady who gives out candy on Halloween, and that's okay, but there's so much more to being kind than that. Kindness is not just for the old or the young; it's for everyone. Kindness is all around us –it's the quiet child holding the door open for someone else or the person who lets friends borrow their clothes. It's how you comfort a friend when they're sad or share your favorite toy with a new friend. Being kind is not just about being nice; it's about being thoughtful. Kindness lets people know that you care, and what could be better than that?

Kindness is a mindset. Being kind means thinking before you act. That way, when you do something nice, it's not just a spur-of-the-moment thing. It's your way of showing people they are worth your time and attention. It's just like being a superhero.

Why is being kind super important? There are many reasons, but one, in particular, you should always remember: kindness makes the world better. Just think about it: They will feel loved and appreciated when you do something kind for someone. This will inspire them to be kind, too, and then they will do something kind for someone else and spread that kindness worldwide. Pretty neat, huh?

There is no doubt that kindness leads to happiness. It's true. People who are kind to others have stronger personal relationships, friendships, and communities. Kind people also tend to have higher self-esteem and better motivation for things. However, it's not just the kind person who is better off; it's *everyone involved.* Think about how great you feel when someone does something nice for you. Kindness creates happiness all over, whether it be the person being kind or the person being helped.

Super Kind Quiz

Take this quiz and find out if you are super kind or still have some work to do. If you answer yes to most of these questions, you are on your way to being a master of kindness. For a better score, always help others, even when it's not easy (or when people don't even notice).

1. Are you thoughtful about the things you say to others?
2. Do you help put away the groceries even when your mom doesn't ask you to?
3. Do you help shovel out your neighbors' walkways when it's snowing outside?
4. Do you pick up trash in your neighborhood even when you're wearing your favorite shirt?
5. Do you treat people differently from you (like people with disabilities) just like everyone else?
6. Do you greet everyone with a smile at school, even if they are strangers or don't seem nice?
7. When someone asks for help, do you stop what you're doing and lend a hand?
8. Have you ever put other people's needs before your own?
9. Have you ever noticed when someone isn't feeling well and tried to make them feel better?
10. If someone's dog is loose while you're outside, do you go out of your way to bring it back?
11. When your friend is having a bad day, do you tell them jokes or stories to cheer them up?
12. Have you ever volunteered at places like a children's hospital or an animal shelter?
13. Are you a good listener who doesn't interrupt others when they are talking?
14. If someone is being treated unfairly, do you stick up for them?
15. Are you kind to animals?

So, what did you score? If you scored at least 9 out of the 15 questions right, then you are a super kind person who should be proud! However, if you scored lower than that, don't feel bad. You can still be one of the most memorable superheroes in your community by just trying a little harder. If you want to be super kind but aren't sure, remember these three tips:

- **Be Polite**

Remember always to say please and thank you, and be aware of the tone you use when talking to others. You will get along with everyone better by being polite, from the person running the register at your favorite store to the janitor at school.

- **Remember How It Feels When Someone Is Nice to You**

Have you ever had someone compliment you or do something nice for you? Remember that feeling and carry it with you throughout the day. Also, remember how it feels when someone is unkind to you, like when someone sneezes on your sandwich. Keep that feeling with you, then choose who you want to be.

- **Be Nice Even if No One Notices**

If you do something nice for someone, but they don't say "thank you" or notice, don't let it bother you. Being a superhero is about doing the right thing even when no one notices. It doesn't matter if anyone sees your kind acts. What matters is that you're making the world a better place.

KINDNESS TREE

Give a Compliment

Help make a meal

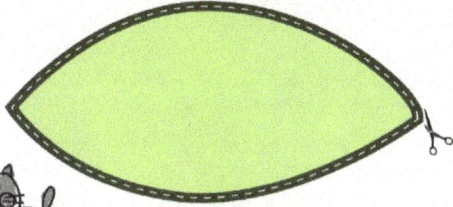

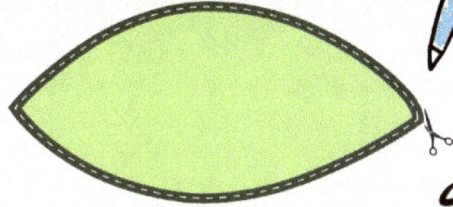

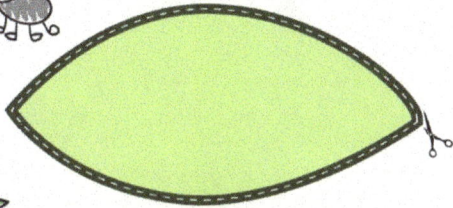

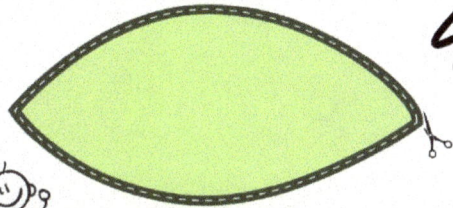

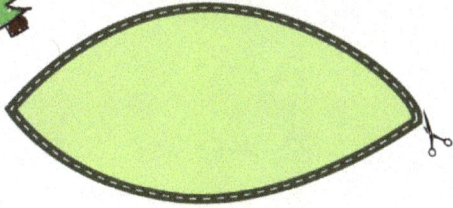

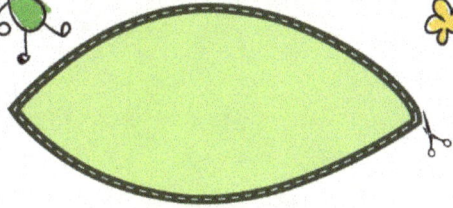

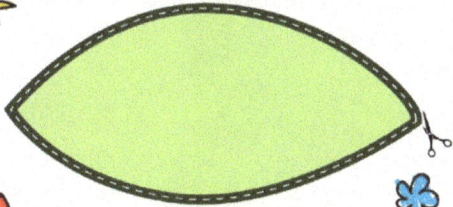

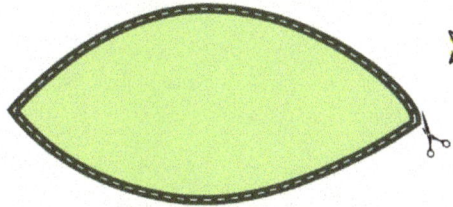

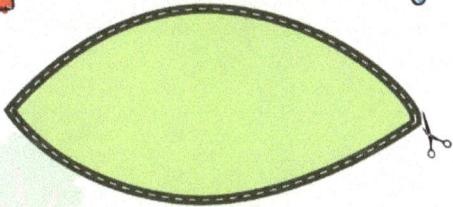

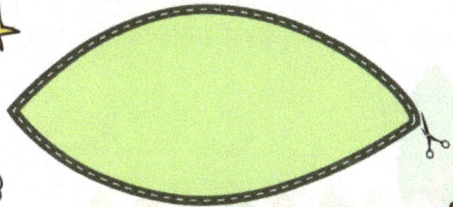

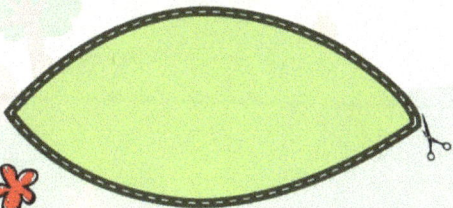

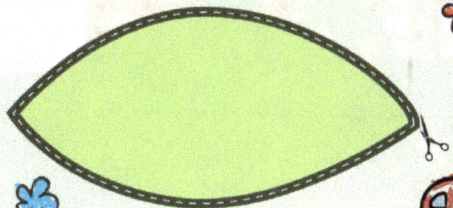

Exercises

The Kindness Calendar

This one is straightforward. Place a little tick on a calendar every day when you are kind. It'll just take a few minutes and will definitely make you feel better about yourself.

January 2024

Sunday	Monday	Tuesday	Wednesday	Thursday	Friday	Saturday
	1	2	3	4	5	6
7	8	9	10	11	12	13
14	15	16	17	18	19	20
21	22	23	24	25	26	27
28	29	30	31			

February 2024

Sunday	Monday	Tuesday	Wednesday	Thursday	Friday	Saturday
				1	2	3
4	5	6	7	8	9	10
11	12	13	14	15	16	17
18	19	20	21	22	23	24
25	26	27	28	29		

March 2024

Sunday	Monday	Tuesday	Wednesday	Thursday	Friday	Saturday
					1	2
3	4	5	6	7	8	9
10	11	12	13	14	15	16
17	18	19	20	21	22	23
24 / 31	25	26	27	28	29	30

April 2024

Sunday	Monday	Tuesday	Wednesday	Thursday	Friday	Saturday
	1	2	3	4	5	6
7	8	9	10	11	12	13
14	15	16	17	18	19	20
21	22	23	24	25	26	27
28	29	30				

May 2024

Sunday	Monday	Tuesday	Wednesday	Thursday	Friday	Saturday
			1	2	3	4
5	6	7	8	9	10	11
12	13	14	15	16	17	18
19	20	21	22	23	24	25
26	27	28	29	30	31	

June 2024

Sunday	Monday	Tuesday	Wednesday	Thursday	Friday	Saturday
2	3	4	5	6	7	8
9	10	11	12	13	14	15
16	17	18	19	20	21	22
23 30	24	25	26	27	28	29

July 2024

Sunday	Monday	Tuesday	Wednesday	Thursday	Friday	Saturday
	1	2	3	4	5	6
7	8	9	10	11	12	13
14	15	16	17	18	19	20
21	22	23	24	25	26	27
28	29	30	31			

August 2024

Sunday	Monday	Tuesday	Wednesday	Thursday	Friday	Saturday
				1	2	3
4	5	6	7	8	9	10
11	12	13	14	15	16	17
18	19	20	21	22	23	24
25	26	27	28	29	30	31

September 2024

Sunday	Monday	Tuesday	Wednesday	Thursday	Friday	Saturday
1	2	3	4	5	6	7
8	9	10	11	12	13	14
15	16	17	18	19	20	21
22	23	24	25	26	27	28
29	30					

October 2024

Sunday	Monday	Tuesday	Wednesday	Thursday	Friday	Saturday
		1	2	3	4	5
6	7	8	9	10	11	12
13	14	15	16	17	18	19
20	21	22	23	24	25	26
27	28	29	30	31		

November 2024

Sunday	Monday	Tuesday	Wednesday	Thursday	Friday	Saturday
					1	2
3	4	5	6	7	8	9
10	11	12	13	14	15	16
17	18	19	20	21	22	23
24	25	26	27	28	29	30

December 2024

Sunday	Monday	Tuesday	Wednesday	Thursday	Friday	Saturday
1	2	3	4	5	6	7
8	9	10	11	12	13	14
15	16	17	18	19	20	21
22	23	24	25	26	27	28
29	30	31				

The Kindness Journal

At the end of every day, write about all the ways you were kind. Make sure to include a description of what happened, what it felt like, and why you did it.

The Superhero Jar

Do something kind every day –it could be anything from helping someone carry their groceries home to offering help to someone with their homework to sharing something of yours with them. Write down all the nice things you do each day and put them in a jar. Tell your parents about this bright idea, and they might exchange your full jar for a special gift at Christmas.

Make a Kindness Chain

You'll need some friends for this one. Each person shares a story about kindness from that day and then passes the chain to the next person in line. By the time it gets to the last person, everyone has heard lots of great stories –and how kind everyone else was. Also, you might hear about the most interesting adventures that inspire you to be even kinder!

A KINDNESS CHALLENGE

PICK UP LITTER IN THE PARK	SAY THANK YOU TO YOUR TEACHERS	GIVE SOMEONE A FLOWER	DO A SIBLING'S CHORE
SMILE AT EVERYONE YOU SEE TODAY	LET SOMEONE GO AHEAD OF YOU IN LINE	GIVE SOMEONE A HUG	CREATE A CARE PACKAGE
PICK A FEW TOYS TO DONATE	PLAY WITH SOMEONE NEW	CLEAN UP WITHOUT BEING ASKED	DONATE A CAN OF FOOD
COMPLIMENT 5 PEOPLE TODAY	HOLD THE DOOR FOR SOMEONE	WRITE A THANK YOU LETTER	OFFER TO HELP A FRIEND

Set a goal of upgrading how kind you are -more smiles, compliments, and helpfulness. Do at least one kind thing a day and see how you feel.

Random Acts of Kindness

Are you ready to spread kindness like confetti? Here's how you can make the world a brighter place:

- **Write a kind note:** Take a few minutes to write a sweet note or draw a picture for a friend, family member, or teacher. As a sweet surprise, leave it somewhere they'll find it.

- **Help a neighbor:** Offer to help your neighbor with something small, like watering their plants, taking out their trash, or walking their dog. They'll really appreciate it.

- **Share a smile:** Smile at strangers you pass by on the street or even at the mall. You shouldn't talk to strangers, but you can smile when you look at them. A friendly smile can brighten someone's day and make them feel noticed and valued.

- **Hold the door open:** When you see someone approaching a door behind you, hold it open and let them go first. It's a simple act of courtesy that shows you care about people.

- **Donate old toys:** Gather some toys or books you no longer use and donate them to a local shelter or charity. Somebody will be very happy to have them.

- **Set the table:** Surprise your family by setting the table for dinner without being asked. It shows that you're thoughtful and willing to help out around the house.

Kindness is what makes the world go round. You may have heard the phrase, "It's better to give than to receive." That's probably because giving feels awesome – it gives you a sense of accomplishment and makes you feel like you are a good person. Remember that superheroes are not born. They are made, and you can start being the greatest superhero you know by taking a few simple steps toward kindness every day.

Chapter 4: Build Self Confidence

The Power of Confidence

Imagine waking up every morning feeling like a rock star, ready to do absolutely anything. That's what confidence does for you. It helps you feel strong, brave, and capable. With confidence, you can try new things, face your fears, and discover talents you didn't even know you had. When you believe in yourself, others also start to believe in you. Your confidence acts like a magnet that attracts people who admire your positive attitude. It helps you make new friends, do great in school, and have the most exciting adventures.

Even if something seems hard at first, confidence helps you keep trying and learning until you succeed. Not only that, but it also makes you happy and proud of who you are. It's like a big high-five to yourself. When you're confident, you feel less worried or scared because you know deep down that you are special and amazing, *just the way you are.*

A confident person knows they're good at what they do. They know what they can and can't do, and their goals align with their abilities. A well-balanced mindset helps them meet challenges head-on with complete belief in themselves and a clear understanding of what success looks like.

Feeling good about yourself can help you inspire others.
https://pixabay.com/photos/say-yes-to-the-live-pleasure-2121044/

When you feel good about yourself, you're more open to sharing your talents with others, and when your skills inspire others, it can really help build a strong sense of self-trust and self-confidence. Many people want to feel this way more often, but it's not always easy. They say self-confidence comes from within, but what exactly are the steps to reaching into yourself and pulling it out? There are many ways to do it, but here are four main strategies that are a sure bet:

Goal Setting

A Quick Fact for You: You can change your brain's shape through neuroplasticity. This is the ability of the brain's neurons to grow new connections or strengthen existing ones. Neurons are like wires that transport electrical messages throughout the body. These special wires can grow new branches or even die and be replaced with new ones. This is part of how the brain changes over time and how you go from not knowing something to knowing something. Defining your goals and working towards them helps your brain create a clear map of "what's possible," and once you know what you want your life to look like, your brain has an easier time getting you there. A goal is something you really want to do, and sometimes, it can take a long time for you to finally do it. These are called long-term goals. A good example is learning to play an instrument and perfect your skills. Short-term goals, on the other hand, happen much quicker, but they're just as important as long-term goals. When you accomplish short-term goals, you get a big boost in confidence because you just did something you really wanted to do, making you feel good about yourself and your skills.

Activity: To practice goal setting, make a list of everything you should do in a day and cross them off the list as you do them. Your list can include everything from brushing your teeth to bathing your dog or practicing the piano. At the end of every day, look at your list and congratulate yourself for all the things you accomplished.

Practice Makes Better

You'll have a much easier time living in a body you're proud of if you know how the body works. You can't do something well if you don't figure out how it works, like learning to do a backflip or learning to dance. As they say, condition your body, and your muscles will respond, so the more you practice something, the better you get at it and the more confident you will feel.

Activity: Practice something important to you, like learning a song or memorizing a poem. Do it in front of a mirror at first, and then do it around other people. You'll be performing so well in no time that people will be impressed with what you can do.

Embrace Your Uniqueness

You are one of a kind. There are no two people in the world who are exactly the same, and it's because of this that everyone is special. Whether it's something really big like being a great athlete or something small like having the ability to make people laugh, everyone has something unique about them to be proud of.

Activity: Think about the things you're good at and find ways to use those skills at least once a day. Maybe you're really good at telling jokes, or maybe you can draw really well, or you can dance like nobody's business. Whatever it is, play around with it and feel special about it.

Learn from Your Mistakes

Experimenting and failing can help you learn faster and build self-confidence. It's like a muscle. The more you use it, the stronger it becomes. Trying something new and failing at it is normal, but don't just give up on something when you make a mistake. Instead, think about what went wrong and correct it when you try again.

Activity: Next time you fail at something, pick yourself up and try again. Maybe you didn't pass a test, so try again. Maybe you didn't do the dishes properly. Try again. Or maybe you were singing in public, and it didn't go so well. Try again. If you need to, ask for help, but always consider trying again.

There you have it for building self-confidence. Start by setting goals, practicing your skills often, learning from your mistakes, and always embracing your uniqueness. Your brain will take a while to learn all these things, but the more you do it, the easier it will become – and the more confident you will feel.

Exercises

Create a Vision Board

A vision board is a tool for goal setting. It is made of words and pictures related to what you want to do. It's the perfect place to display your dreams, ideas, and strengths. These boards can also be used to remind you how you've achieved those goals, which can motivate you to keep going. The great thing about vision boards is that the goals don't all have to be serious. They can be funny or silly – *as long as they matter to you.* Ask your parents to help you create your vision board, or you can do it with your friends. All you'll need is a big piece of poster board, glue, scissors, and pictures from magazines. You can also use words cut out of magazines or newspapers or write the word yourself on the board.

Something New, Something Cool

This activity will have you exploring who you are, what you're interested in, and what you want to be. Cut paper into small pieces and write down things you've never done but want to try on each one. Place the papers in a box, and each week, you pick a piece of paper and do whatever the paper says. Remember that the point isn't to be cool or popular but rather to be YOU, so don't be afraid to try something new.

Affirmations Jar

Affirmations are positive things you say to yourself to feel better and build your self-confidence. Write down a list of affirmations on small pieces of paper. Here are some examples: I am beautiful, I am loved, I am smart, etc. Put the pieces of paper in a jar, and each day, take one out and read it. Saying it to yourself can help you believe it's true. Affirmations don't have to be specific. They can be about anything you want them to be or even about something you're trying to achieve.

You have your whole life in front of you. The future can be whatever you want it to be, and if you believe you can do it, chances are really good that you will succeed. Building self-confidence is a process, so don't get discouraged if it takes some time to get the hang of it. Just keep practicing, and one day, you'll look back and realize that you are living as confidently as you've always dreamed.

Chapter 5: Winning and Losing

Losing can be really tough. Most times, it hurts your feelings. Other times, you're mad at yourself because you feel you didn't try hard enough, and sometimes people around you say mean things like 'you got beat' or 'loser' (or worse). Winning, though, feels awesome! You're proud of yourself and get to share in the spotlight with your friends and teammates. Everyone likes to win. A secret, however, is that winning isn't everything. It is a good thing, but sometimes there are better things. What could possibly be better than winning, you say? Well, winning means you tried. It means you were up for the game -not late, sick, left out, or a wimp. You participated. If you're out for fun, it doesn't matter if you lose. The joy of playing the game and giving it your all is just as rewarding as coming out on top.

Everyone likes to win.
https://pixabay.com/illustrations/what-is-the-memorial-awards-trophies-2841755/

It's about the journey, the effort, and the growth that comes from pushing yourself and the improvement that comes with it. Sometimes, the lessons learned from a loss are more valuable than the short-lived satisfaction of a victory. Losing teaches you how to cope when things are hard. It teaches you to be humble and not give up. It forces you to reflect on your mistakes, learn from them, and come back stronger. In fact, some of the biggest stars in the world have incredible stories of losing and coming back stronger.

Take Michael Jordan, for example. Before becoming the basketball legend he is known as today, Jordan had a hard time and lost a lot. He was cut from his high school basketball team and failed at many other things he tried, like baseball and football. However, instead of giving up, Jordan used this rejection as fuel to work harder and prove himself. He practiced longer and harder until he became one of the greatest basketball players ever.

Michael Jordan is just one example. There's also Albert Einstein, who failed over and over again in school as a child. He had to work harder to catch up with his classmates, and he would go home tired every night. Yet he didn't give up. Instead, he kept trying, and today, he is known as one of the greatest minds that ever lived. J.K. Rowling, one of the most successful writers and billionaires around today, was turned down by 12 publishers before anyone would even look at her first Harry Potter book. Her story is one of loss and rejection. She had to rewrite her book several times before it was finally picked up, but in the end, it made her a household name and a bestselling author all over the world.

You'd be surprised at how many great people had to work really hard or hear 'no' a lot before they got where they are today. If they can do it, so can you. It's not about winning or losing. It's about using the experience to make you a better person and help you learn from your mistakes. So next time you lose, don't get mad at yourself for making mistakes. Learn from it and say, "I did my best. I tried my hardest. Maybe I can do even better next time."

Famous Quotes About Winning and Losing

"Winning doesn't always mean being first. Winning means you're doing better than you've ever done before." - Bonnie Blair

"The measure of who we are is how we react after a loss." - Serena Williams

"The greatest glory in living lies not in never falling, but in rising every time we fall." - Nelson Mandela

"You have to learn how to lose before you can win." - Kareem Abdul-Jabbar

"Winning is great, sure, but if you are really going to do something in life, the secret is learning how to lose." - Wilma Rudolph

"Success is not final, failure is not fatal: it is the courage to continue that counts." - Winston Churchill

"The harder the battle, the sweeter the victory." - Les Brown

"Winning is only half of it. Having fun is the other half." - Bum Phillips

"I've missed more than 9,000 shots in my career. I've lost almost 300 games. Twenty-six times, I've been trusted to take the game-winning shot and missed. I've failed over and over and over again in my life. And that is why I succeed." - Michael Jordan

"You can never lose if you never give up." - Babe Ruth

Coping Skills

A coping skill will help you get through a hard time, like when you're sad or angry. It doesn't make the hurt go away, but it can help you think about your problem differently or handle it better. Coping skills are great because they help you feel better without hurting others. Here are some coping skills you can try next time you don't feel so good:

1. **Write down how you feel.** Writing about a problem can make you feel better. Sometimes, just getting all your feelings out somehow makes it easier to move on and stop feeling bad.

2. **Hug someone you love who loves you back.** Hugging will make you feel better, and it has no side effects, except maybe for a bone-crushing hug from your dad!

3. **If you're not in much pain or upset, laugh about the problem.** Sometimes, when you're really sad, you feel like you'll never laugh again. Remember a time when you laughed a lot, even if it was a long time ago? Remembering how it felt to laugh can help you feel happier.

4. **Help someone else.** Next time you feel like there's no way out, find someone else who needs your help and make their situation better. You'll forget about feeling sad or angry when you're doing something nice for someone else.

5. **Count to ten.** When you get mad, it's easy to say or do things that hurt others, even if you didn't mean to. So if you start to feel mad, count slowly in your head from one to ten and try to relax. It might not work right away, but it's always worth a shot.

6. **Let yourself be sad when you need to be.** You don't always have to act super strong, even though it may seem like the popular thing to do. Sometimes, you need to cry and let out all those sad feelings. It's not a big deal, and in most cases, it will make you feel better.

Exercises

1. **"What Do I Do?":** Get your mom or dad to help you with this game. All they need to do is come up with random scenarios where you feel stuck, sad, or angry about losing and then ask, "What do you do?" For example, "You didn't get a high score on the quiz, even though you studied really hard. What do you do?" "You tried out for the basketball team, but your shot isn't as good as you thought. What do you do?" "You didn't get picked to be part of the school play. What do you do?" They can be as creative and weird as they want, and the more difficult or impossible the scenario, the better you will get at coming up with positive solutions.

2. **Happy Thoughts:** This exercise is for times when your sadness or anger is big, and you feel like you can do nothing about it. Instead of letting yourself feel that way, try being happy about something else. Get a sheet of paper and a marker. Draw a line down the middle to divide it into two halves. At the top of one half, write "Sad," and at the top of the second half, write "Lucky." Write down what you're feeling in the Sad section and all the lucky things about you or your life in the Lucky section. When you're done, compare the two lists. The idea is that even though you're upset right now, there is always something good that you can be grateful for.

3. **Three Lessons:** This great exercise helps you turn every situation into a learning experience. Ask yourself, "What lesson can I learn from this?" and then write down three really good answers. Writing it down brings it to life. For example, if you can't do something you want to do, ask yourself what lessons are hidden inside that issue. Maybe it's about patience or trying

something else. Or maybe it's about asking someone else for help. Even when you win, lessons are still to be learned because it's not about winning at all. It's about learning and growing, so this exercise is great for both wins and losses.

4. **Sportsmanship Award**: Most of the time, competitive sports can be too serious and intense, especially for kids your age. So, instead of focusing on winning, how about focusing on being kind to people and having a good time? To make this exercise work, you'll need to get your friends or family involved, and you all can make a supercool sportsmanship award for the person who shows the most teamwork, courtesy, and best attitude of all, whether they win or lose. It's nice to be proud of something that doesn't involve winning. Before you know it, the trend will catch on, and you might get one from someone else.

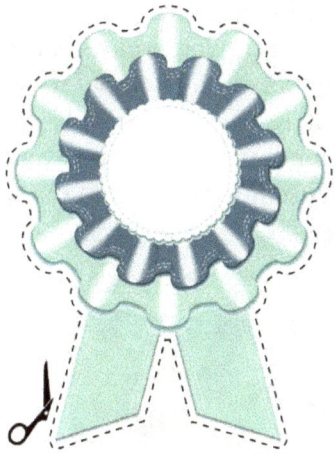

Chapter 6: Listening and Paying Attention

Are you a good listener? Do you know what it means to *truly listen?* It's normal to think that listening means simply hearing the other person talk, but that's only half the truth. Listening is not just about hearing words. It is about listening to the tone of someone's voice and observing non-verbal cues like facial expressions, mannerisms, and body language for signs of how the person feels about what they're saying and what they might be thinking. It means showing genuine interest in what people are saying and thinking carefully about what you hear. Listening means paying attention. When you pay attention, you take in as much information as you can from the conversation and use it to respond to the speaker.

Listening means paying attention to what others are saying.

Not everyone is a great listener. You may think that the other person should be able to tell when you're not paying attention and interrupt or say something to make you pay attention, but sometimes people are too polite to say anything when they realize you're not listening. Or maybe they think that they are boring you or that you have a lot on your mind. If this happens a lot, people might start to think that you don't care about them and stop talking to you about important things. You don't want to be left out of the important stuff, do you?

Are You a Good Listener?

How do you know if you're a good listener? Here are some clues.

- You are focused on the other person and what they are saying
- You listen with your ears, eyes, mouth, and mind. (This means keeping your mouth closed when the other person is speaking and using your eyes, head, and body to show that you are paying attention).
- You have good eye contact. You might think that staring straight at the other person can be rude, but it's just one way to show people that you're interested in what they're saying. (You can also glance at them from time to time).
- You ensure the other person knows you're listening. (You can nod, smile, or comment to show them that you understand what they're saying).
- You ask questions, showing that you're genuinely interested in what they say.
- People enjoy talking to you.

If you agree that most of these are true about you, then you're probably a good listener! People will enjoy talking to you and sharing their thoughts. However, if some of these aren't true for you, don't worry. Everything has a learning curve. You can learn to be a good listener by practicing with the people around you. Anyone can get better at listening, and you are no different.

Why Listening Matters

Listening not only shows respect for the other person but also impacts your relationship and your ability to connect. The person will know that their opinions matter to you, and they will want to hang out with you more. Being a good listener means:

- People are more likely to share things with you if they know you will listen.
- When people feel comfortable talking about things that matter to them, they are more likely to share personal information. This makes it easier for you to learn about them and find out what's important to them. Knowing this information can help you understand how they think and see the world.
- When people feel that you listen to them, they respect you more.
- If people are feeling down, they will tell you, and you'll be able to help. Listening makes them feel better because it shows them that you care about what is going on in their lives.
- You can help people because they'll tell you exactly what they need, whether directly or indirectly.
- Good listening skills are key to managing your time and staying organized. You will be better able to remember the important things people tell you if you listen closely.

Listening can also help you in school. You'll be able to:

- Learn more when you pay attention in class.
- Study better when you have meaningful information.
- Understand what teachers and other adults want from you. This will help your grades go up!
- Make connections between what you're learning at school and your outside interests, whether sports, music, or books.
- Remember what you've learned, which makes studying for tests easier.
- Keep up-to-date with current events or news that's happening around you. You won't miss anything important!
- Build friendships and connect with the people you care about, especially at school.

Paying attention is a skill that anyone can get better at with practice. You can improve your relationships and make new friends by working on your listening skills. You'll feel better about yourself and be more confident in your ability to connect with others, no matter the situation.

Tips to Become a Good Listener

- Try not to let your mind wander. If you catch yourself thinking about something else, bring yourself back to the conversation by asking a question that focuses on what the other person is saying. Keep yourself alert by saying "yes" and nodding or making eye contact.
- Pay attention to how the other person feels. Are they angry, sad, or happy? You can tell by looking at their face and body language. Then, you can ask follow-up questions that are relevant to their feelings.
- If it's hard for you to pay attention, look away from the other person for a few seconds and take three deep breaths. Try to calm yourself down. Once you feel more relaxed, look at the person again and pay attention.
- If you're having trouble thinking of something to say, ask a question about what the other person is saying. It will show that you are listening and interested in learning more.
- When you need to say something, wait until the other person has finished talking.
- Take notes if you can. Writing things down will help you remember the conversation.
- If you're listening and not saying much, say something now and then, even if it's just "uh huh" or "I see." Say something every few minutes to show the person you're talking to that they have your undivided attention.
- If you're unsure what to say, try rephrasing what the other person said.
- Pay attention to body language. Sometimes, a person's mouth says one thing, but their face is saying another.
- Good listening means slow listening. Answer questions or respond to what someone says slowly and without rushing. This will signal that you are paying attention.

Exercises

1. **Listening Quiz:** Test your listening skills with a fun quiz! Ask a friend or family member to read a short story or set of instructions, and then see how much you can remember and understand. They will throw questions at you, and you will have to answer as accurately as you can. This will help you practice active listening and improve your memory and recall skills.

2. **Body Language Detective:** In this exercise, you will become a body language detective and learn to interpret nonverbal cues (body language). Find a partner and take turns observing each other's body language. Pay attention to facial expressions, gestures, and posture, and try to guess what emotions or messages they might be sending you. This activity will improve your empathy and understanding of others, allowing you to better respond to their needs and feelings.

3. **Paraphrasing Practice:** When paraphrasing, you repeat what someone has said to you to ensure you understand them correctly. Try this out with a friend and see who can do it best. Let your partner say something, and then repeat what they said in your own words. If done well, both of your sentences should mean the same thing. This exercise will help you pay more attention to what others are saying and allow you to respond with greater understanding.

Chapter 7: Sharing Your Opinion and Having Respect

Opinions are a funny thing. When we're confident enough in them, we want to share them with the world, but in the moment, they can change –sometimes drastically. On the other hand, when we're not confident, we keep our opinions to ourselves and stay away from conflict. What does it mean to share an opinion, and how should you go about sharing that opinion without causing conflict or hurting someone's feelings? It can be easy to ruin a conversation (and the message in your opinion) by being insensitive, forceful, or cold. You want to share your opinions while still keeping the respect you owe others.

Some people think sharing their opinion means shouting it from the rooftops to whoever will listen, but that's not sharing an opinion. It's telling. When you tell someone your opinion, you don't allow them any say in the matter. Telling isn't sharing; it's forcing. "There's a difference between opinion and attitude," says Allie Brosh, an American humorist, in her book Roughing It. "When you have an attitude, you're attacking someone else's way of life because you think yours is better."

Share your opinion, but do it with the right tone. Maybe you're making a point that's personal or sharing a thought that makes you angry or upset. A cold and forceful opinion could come across as threatening or rude, but an even colder, more rude opinion won't get the point across. You may be right, but if your comment comes off like it's meant to be forceful or mean, then you might have some trouble getting people on your side. Find the right balance. You want to share an opinion but make it easy for others to share their opinions.

It can be hard to know how to express your opinion and keep a respectful tone, especially if you wholeheartedly believe in what you stand for. The best advice here is to soften the blow a little. Instead of telling someone they're wrong, explain why you feel that way. Help others understand your point of view. When you're sharing what you think, there is a chance that someone else might disagree with you, and that's okay. You aren't going to agree with everyone all the time either, and that's fine.

Respect is the key to sharing your opinion with others while still keeping them comfortable with your message. When you respect others, you show that you are aware of their presence and that they have the right to exist in the world, no matter what that might mean for your opinion. When you share an opinion, let it be respectfully expressed, and have faith that others will do the same for you.

The Value of Respect

Respect is something you earn, not something that's given. When you respect others and their opinions, you create a space for healthy, productive communication. Respect is the give-and-take that allows everyone to share their ideas without risking being misunderstood or treated unfairly. People should feel safe expressing their opinions in the company of others who understand their differences and want to hear them out and have a chance to form an opinion of their own.

There are hundreds of ways to express your opinion respectfully, but it all begins with respecting how other people see things. When you respect someone, you'll keep your tone friendly, even when sharing an unpopular opinion. You can respect someone without agreeing with them, and that's okay! Respectful disagreement is the cornerstone of our free society, and when you respect someone, you acknowledge their right to hold opinions different from your own. Personal opinions can change over time, and what's right for you won't always be right for everyone.

Respect is something you have for yourself, too. It is your duty to be true to yourself and your beliefs. Self-respect is a powerful tool that comes with many benefits. It gives you the confidence to share your opinions, even if they differ from what others say. It helps you listen to, understand, and learn from the people around you. It makes it easier for you to understand what others think and know how to express that understanding in a way that is respectful of them but also true to yourself.

Respect is how you treat everyone you meet, from the people you live with to those you meet online. It is not only how you speak to your friends and family but also to strangers. It's how you make your voice heard in the world without making anyone feel bad or threatened by what you have to say.

Respect is important because it can stop fights before they begin. When we respect the thoughts of others, we can avoid many arguments by listening and accepting what others say without feeling the need to win the argument. In a world where people disagree on many things, respect is more necessary than ever. When we stop passing judgment and see that everyone has something to contribute, we can strike up amazing conversations with anyone, anywhere.

Tips for Sharing Your Opinion Respectfully

Listen

When you listen to the opinions of others, you can choose to agree or disagree, but at least you'll have learned something new, no matter your choice. Many people have no trouble speaking their minds but have a harder time listening. The best way to practice sharing your opinion is to listen.

Respect the Other Person's Feelings

When sharing your opinion, remember that it's okay for someone else not to agree with you. Each person has a right to his or her opinion. Be respectful when presenting your ideas and opinions, making people more comfortable sharing theirs.

Be Authentic

When you're sharing your own opinion, be honest. Don't say things just to get a reaction; if you do that, your words won't carry any weight. Being genuine helps others respect you and helps you respect yourself.

Exercises

1. **Role-Play:** One way to practice sharing your opinions is through role-playing exercises. This allows you to step into different roles and practice expressing your thoughts in a safe and controlled environment. You can assign different roles to other players and engage in a debate or talk about a specific topic. This will improve your communication skills, but that's not all. It will also teach you the importance of respecting different viewpoints. On top of that, role-playing is a fun and interactive way for you and your friends to explore your creativity and imagination.

2. **Respect Circle:** Another way to practice sharing your opinions is the Respect Circle. In this exercise, all the players sit in a circle and take turns sharing their thoughts and opinions on any chosen topic. The key is to listen attentively to the other players without interrupting or judging. This way, everyone feels heard and valued, encouraging a sense of respect and understanding among the group. As the players trade their views, they should hold the other person's opinions seriously and not make any negative judgments about them. This will help you get used to the idea that, even though your opinion may be different, it's no less valid than anyone else's.

3. **Empathy Drawing:** This exercise teaches you to put yourself in another person's shoes. To start, have all the players sit in a circle. Everyone takes turns speaking and expressing their opinion on any topic of their choice. The other players in the circle will then draw pictures that show how they think the speaker feels. When that's done, they will share their drawings with the rest of the group, and the speaker can then say if their feelings were accurately represented and if there were any elements or details they missed. This exercise is a great way to practice expressing your opinions in a respectful way, as well as helping you understand the other person's viewpoint.

4. **The Scavenger Hunt:** This interactive game allows players to actively seek out examples of respectful behavior in their surroundings. You can do this on your own or get a team together. The goal is to find as many instances of respect as possible within a given period. This exercise encourages you to be observant and aware of your surroundings and makes you reflect on the

importance of respect in everyday interactions. It can be a fun and engaging way for you to see respect in action.

INDOOR SCAVENGER HUNT

How many of these items can you find around the house?

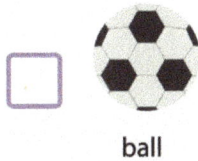

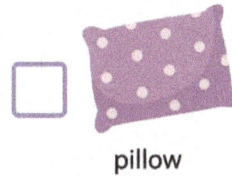

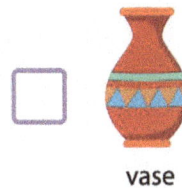

☐ book

☐ gloves

☐ pan

☐ ball

☐ juice

☐ pillow

☐ glasses

☐ jewelry

☐ telephone

☐ balloon

☐ key

☐ toy

☐ lemon

☐ ring

☐ vase

☐ umbrella

☐ lamp

☐ socks

Respect must be learned and cultivated over time. The best way to learn it is through experience and practice, but you can start now by recognizing when people go out of their way to show respect to you and everyone around them. Practice sharing your opinions, and ensure you're listening to everyone who wants to share theirs. By understanding what respect means, you'll be able to grow from experience and show those around you what it looks like.

Chapter 8: Digital Manners: Being Nice Online

The internet is a wonderful place, but it's not always great. Sometimes, you find yourself the target of rude comments or worse. No matter your age, you should be aware of some simple digital etiquette so you and your friends can avoid being the target of trolls. A troll is someone who intentionally provokes other people, usually for the sake of humor or entertainment. It's a person on the internet who will go out of their way to say something rude or hurtful to make people mad. At its worst, this is emotionally damaging and can lead to other problems, such as cyberbullying.

Bad internet behavior can have negative consequences.
https://pixabay.com/photos/children-win-success-video-game-593313/

You can get hurt by this all-too-common internet behavior or hurt someone yourself. Online courtesy is a must to keep you and your friends safe and happy. Without it, you'll be lost in a pile of comments ranging from annoying to downright mean. Here are the top five reasons you should follow online etiquette:

It Will Make You Feel and Look Better

There are more than seven billion people on earth and over three billion on planet Twitter alone. Obviously, many of them are adults rather than children, but there is no reason for anyone to speak to you unkindly, especially if you did nothing to bring it upon yourself. When you tweet, blog, or post on Facebook, ask yourself, "What would I say to a friend in similar circumstances?" Most people are more forgiving of people they know and understanding of their mistakes than they are of complete strangers whom they've never met before. It may not be within your power to change that person's behavior and make them nicer, but it is within your power to show kindness towards them regardless.

It Will Make Life Easier

The more you treat people badly, the more likely they'll get back at you. People who always have something nasty to say about others are usually not very popular themselves and often end up alone. Younger people often don't realize how easily they can be tracked down if their "anonymity" is stripped away online and how quickly news travels through the internet. With the ever-present possibility of being tracked and caught, being nice online is smart.

You Will Find Friends with Whom You Can Be Your Genuine Self

This issue applies not only to younger people but to adults as well. If you tweet or chat in offensive and uncalled-for ways, you've likely lost the opportunity to make new friends. On the flip side, if you tweet or blog with kindness and respect, others will be more inclined to do the same.

It Will Make Your Offline Life Easier

Online rumors can spread like wildfire if left unchecked. That is what it means to go viral. For the right reasons, it can be a good thing. You can become insanely popular quickly if your posts or tweets are seen as helpful, interesting, or funny. However, bad things can go viral just as easily, and if your reputation is completely destroyed, you won't just be hurt but isolated. Those rumors may even threaten your safety. It is always in your best interest to eliminate confusion and hate before it becomes a problem. Today, technology plays such a strong part in our lives that we need to understand how to interact with it. Online etiquette can help you learn how to socialize without fear of being judged and show the world that you know how to treat others with kindness and respect, even if only through words.

It Will Make the World a Better Place for Everyone

One of the best things about your generation is that you are not afraid to speak your mind. People born before you may not have had the same opportunities, but you do. For that, we should all be thankful. Use your voice to spread kindness and knowledge. You don't need to be Mr. or Ms. Nice Guy 100% of the time, but remember that it is better to be nice than mean. Do your part in making the world a better place, one tweet at a time.

Use your devices to spread kindness on the internet.

Digital Etiquette Quiz

If you are in a time crunch or want a little help, here is a short quiz to see how nice you are online. Take this quick quiz and check your score below.

1. I always tell the truth when writing online.

True/False

2. I don't say anything at all if I can't say something nice.

True/False

3. If I see someone being mean online, I ignore it.

True/False

4. I never use online language that is inappropriate or offensive.

True/False

5. If I see someone gossiping on my social media, I ignore it.

True/False

6. I always say "please" and "thank you" when asking for something online.

True/False

7. If someone reports me for stealing content, I apologize right away.

True/False

8. I don't share personal information about friends or family online.

True/False

9. I make sure people are okay with me posting their pictures before I post them online.

True/False

10. When someone reports me for trolling or bullying, I take it as a sign that I need to change my ways and correct my behavior.

True/False

If you answered True to most questions, you are a master of online etiquette. Congratulations on conquering the digital age! However, don't feel bad if you answered True to just two or three questions. It just means that you could be nicer online. Don't worry, there are ways to improve, and you don't have to go it alone. Check out the tips below and use them to brush up on your digital manners.

11 Ways to Be Nicer Online

1. Always speak your mind using words you would be comfortable saying to someone you know. If you wouldn't say it to them, don't post it.

2. You don't need to know everything about everyone right away. Don't be afraid to ask for help if you're not sure how to respond in a given situation.

3. Never share private details about yourself or your friends, and don't be afraid to tell people that they are asking for too much information.

4. Don't take personal attacks on the internet too seriously. Chances are, the person saying these things is just trying to get a rise out of you, and it's not worth getting angry. The things people say online are usually not what they would say in real life, so don't let their words bother you.

5. Realize that your voice and your actions have power. Use them to spread kindness and peace.

6. Assume that everyone can see what you're writing and that there is no such thing as a secret.

7. Avoid getting into flame wars. It's like getting into a bar fight with people you've never met before.

8. Stealing other people's content is bad form and might even be illegal. If you do decide to repost someone else's work, always give credit where credit is due.

9. It can be easy to say things online that you normally wouldn't say in real life. Don't post if you find yourself typing something that feels out of character for you.

10. Be respectful of others' opinions, but don't be afraid to share your own. You don't need to change the way you think just because someone else disagrees with you.

11. Take a break sometimes. Life is made up of many parts, and if you spend all your time online, you won't get to experience the other parts of your life to the fullest. So, know when to go offline, relax, and enjoy what's around you.

Exercises

Your Online Rule Book: Brainstorm and come up with your own online rule book. Creating a set of guidelines for responsible online behavior can be a fun and educational activity for you to do alone or with your family. It can help you define what is right and wrong in the digital world. Each rule should be clear and concise, explaining why this behavior is important to you and the consequences for those who break the rules. This exercise helps you understand the point of digital etiquette and lets you take ownership of your online presence. You can include rules such as being kind and respectful to others, not sharing personal information, and seeking adult supervision when needed. By making and following your own rules, you are taking action and setting a positive example for others.

Spot the Troll: This game helps you recognize and deal with trolls or people who post mean things online. Ask someone in your family or friend group to read a post written by a troll on the internet. Have everyone take turns guessing what kind of person wrote it as you discuss some qualities trolls have. Next, discuss strategies for dealing with trolls, such as not engaging with them, blocking or reporting them, and focusing on a positive online presence. This game helps you become more aware of the presence of trolls and how you respond.

Digital Footprint Scavenger Hunt: In this activity, you and your friends search for traces of your digital footprint online. Start by Googling your own name and see what information comes up. Then, explore social media platforms like Twitter, Instagram, and Facebook to see what information they have about you. Use this activity to see how much information about yourself is on the internet and better understand how to monitor and manage your online presence.

Chapter 9: Etiquette for When Visiting Others

There was a lot of talk about etiquette in the last chapter, but what does it actually mean? Why is it so important? Etiquette is how we behave in society or with a group of people. It is a set of behaviors or courtesies that make others feel respected, comfortable, and welcome. The word etiquette is French and actually means "a ticket" or "a label." Back in the days of kings and queens, people dressed up in fine clothes and wore special jewelry when they met royalty. It was like a ticket that said, "I'm rich and significant." This behavior granted them access to the royal court.

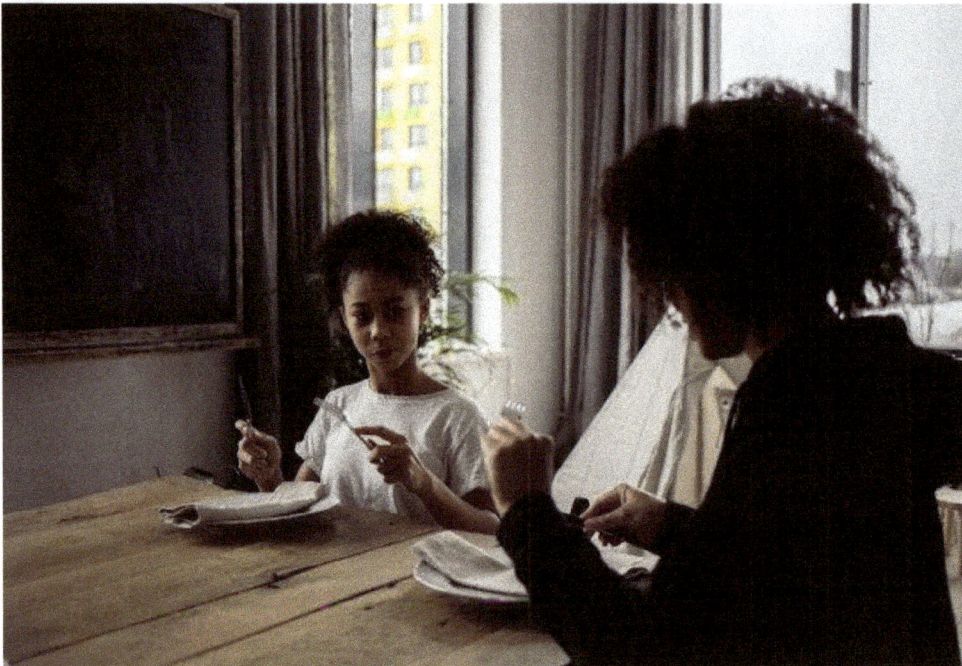

Using etiquette can help you be considerate of other people's feelings.
https://www.pexels.com/photo/black-girl-with-unrecognizable-mother-learning-table-manners-7114102/

Today, we use etiquette as a guide to be polite, friendly, and respectful. This includes being considerate of other people's feelings, paying attention to detail, and using proper manners. There are rules of etiquette for different places and different times. The reason for these rules is to show respect to one another and maintain peace in society. In a classroom or at school, we have school rules that everyone has to follow, just like we do when we are out in public. For example, we must raise our hands before speaking at school. At dinner, when someone makes a suggestion, everyone has to be quiet and listen to see if it is a good idea. We follow these rules because they help us all get along and work together as peacefully as possible. The rules of etiquette also apply when we visit other people's homes, and that's what you'll be learning about in this chapter.

Being a Polite Guest

The first thing to know about being a guest is that you should act like one. When you come to visit others, you should show respect for the way they live and how they do things. You do this by being polite to everyone in the house, saying "please" and "thank you," and trying not to make a mess.

You should always be polite, but people expect you to be on your best behavior when you visit or stay at their house. First impressions are important, and people will judge you as soon as you step through the door. If you act politely and respectfully, they will be more likely to appreciate and treat you well while you're there.

If someone invites you to their house for a meal or a party, it is polite to call them before you go so that they know when to expect you. It is also good manners to warn them if your arrival time is different than the one they were expecting. This shows that you consider their schedule and allow them to make any necessary preparations.

When you arrive at their house, greet them with a warm smile and a friendly hello. This simple act sets a positive tone for the rest of your visit. As you enter their home, be mindful of any house rules or customs they may have. For example, if they ask you to take off your shoes at the door, do so. Some people find it hard to relax in a room full of people who are still wearing their shoes, especially if the guests are wearing muddy or dirty shoes. Respecting their wishes will help you make a good impression.

Showing Gratitude

It is also polite to say "thank you" when people do things that make your stay comfortable or enjoyable, whether offering you food, water, or a place to sit. Some hosts may offer to show you around their house or give you information about it, and it is nice to say thank you for this kindness and service.

It is also good manners to thank people for any presents they give you, even if you don't like them. Think of something honest and nice to say, like, "Thank you so much for this. I really appreciate it." When you receive a gift you don't want or need, smile and say, "Thank you so much. This is so thoughtful of you." You're not lying; you're just being polite.

You can show gratitude by lending a helping hand in some way. For example, if the host asks you to help set the table, go ahead and do it. If they ask for something, like soda or paper plates, offer to get it. You can also offer to help with cleanup at the end of your visit. The more effort you make to show gratitude, the more they will like you and invite you back again.

Etiquette Quiz

How well do you know the rules of etiquette? Take this quick quiz to see whether you've been paying attention.

When entering someone's home, it is polite to:

a) Immediately take off your shoes.

b) Greet the host and thank them for inviting you.

c) Start exploring their house without permission.

True or False: Using your phone or other electronic devices during a meal with others is acceptable.

If someone offers you a gift, it is polite to:

a) Decline the gift.

b) Accept the gift with a genuine thank you.

c) Immediately open the gift in front of them.

True or False: In general, it's polite to help out in any way possible when you visit someone's home.

When visiting someone's house, it is polite to:

a) Bring a gift for them.

b) Offer to help with cleanup even if they say no.

c) Speak loudly and interrupt others who are talking.

True or False: Leaving the table during a meal is considered impolite.

What would you do if the host began a conversation with you?

a) Listen to them and politely respond.

b) Say nothing.

c) Walk away from that conversation at once.

True or False: If someone offers you a seat, it is polite to accept it.

True or False: You should always say "thank you" when someone does something nice for you.

When visiting someone's house, it is polite to:

a) Barge in like you own the place.

b) Help set the table or bring things they are missing from the kitchen.

c) Walk in and start going through their belongings as soon as you walk through the door.

What should you do if a host offers to give you a tour of their home?

a) Accept and say thank you.

b) Refuse so that you can explore the area on your own later.

c) Show appreciation but refuse the offer.

Exercises

House Rules Detective: In this game, you and your friends become detectives and investigate the house rules in your own home or in other places you visit. You can start by observing and making a list of the rules you see, such as taking off shoes at the door or helping with chores. Then, ask your parents or the hosts about any additional rules you may have missed. This activity teaches you proper etiquette and manners and encourages you to be more aware of your surroundings and respect others' spaces.

First Impressions: This activity forces you to think about your goals before you visit someone's house for a gathering. How do you want them to remember you if you go to someone's house? Will you be loud, rude, disrespectful, polite, or kind? It may seem silly, but thinking about these things beforehand can really help.

The Golden Rule: Treat others the way you want to be treated. This classic rule of etiquette can be applied to everyday situations in your home, school, or anywhere else you go. If you are visiting someone's house and want to sit on their couch, would it be better to ask or assume? If you aren't sure, then always ask first.

The Manners Game: In this role-playing game, everyone gets a turn to be the guest and meet the designated host for the first time. From dining etiquette to proper introductions, the players are put to the test as they navigate through a series of challenges designed to showcase their grace, poise, and understanding of social norms. They will be judged not only on their ability to follow the rules of etiquette but also on their ability to adapt to unexpected twists and turns that will appear. The challenges can be silly, serious, or even embarrassing. The goal is to avoid being embarrassed while still making a great impression on your host. This shows how well you know the rules of etiquette and opens up the opportunity for good conversation and laughter while learning.

Etiquette is not just about the rules of what to do and say. It is also about the intentions behind your actions and how to apply them to everyday situations. The goal of etiquette is to make others feel comfortable and relaxed around you so that they don't have to worry about what you will do or how they are supposed to respond. By following these rules of etiquette, you will be much more likely to make a good impression and build up your reputation as someone who is well-mannered, kind, and thoughtful.

Chapter 10: Random Acts of Kindness

A random act of kindness is doing something for another person without any expectation or thought of reward. It can be as big as going out to dinner with someone who lives alone or something small like giving up your seat on the bus for someone with a walker. It is anything that helps someone feel better physically or mentally or helps them in general.

According to a test done by researchers at the University of California, when acts of kindness were performed regularly at work, everyone on the team felt happier, more connected, and more satisfied with their work. The givers admitted to feeling even more satisfaction than the receivers, being happier at work and with life in general.

Another encouraging result from the test was that workers who received acts of kindness were eager to repay them, showing three times more acts of kindness than those who did not receive any acts of kindness. Surprisingly, the acts were not performed out of duty. These workers extended their compassion to people other than the original givers, proving that people, in general, are ready to be part of a generous culture.

You should always be willing to give back, especially to those who are not expecting it. There's a saying that the ripple effects of kindness have no logical end. This means that if you do a kind act, it will trigger others to do the same. Here are a few kind gestures to do for the people around you:

1. **Pass Along a Compliment:** We all want our good qualities to be recognized and appreciated. The next time you see someone and are impressed by something they do, why not let them know?

2. **Clean Up After Yourself:** If it's your turn to clean up after a group project or an outing with friends, don't just leave before you take care of the mess. Clean it up first. It's really not that much extra work, and it helps the next person who does have to do the job.

3. **Make a New Friend:** Almost anyone who finds themselves without a lot of friends will tell you that they wish they had more. You don't need to have an elaborate plan to make new friends. A random act of kindness can be as simple as going up to the new kid in your class and introducing yourself.

4. **Help Out a Cause:** There are a million organizations that help others and need your help. One of the ways to keep your community connected is to help out however you can. Helping them reach their goal will give you a sense of pride in making a difference in someone else's life.

5. **Smile:** It's amazing what a smile can do. When you smile, it puts everyone in a better mood. If someone feels down, give them a genuine smile and cheer them up –it's that easy.

6. **Be Kind to an Animal:** While they may not be able to repay you, animals are living creatures that deserve the same amount of love we do. They can't say thank you, but they sure seem appreciative. Offer them some treats or a toy to play with, and you'll walk away feeling on top of the world.

7. **Give Back to the Elderly:** Before you think that they don't need your help, remember that your grandparents were once kids, too, and they also gave us the gift of life. Offer to help them with something, whether mowing the lawn or walking their dog. It's a great way to give back to the people who raised you.

8. **Help Out Your Community:** Whether cleaning up litter on the side of the road or doing a service project in your neighborhood, the little things can go a long way.

9. **Listen:** One small act of kindness that often gets overlooked is just listening to someone who's upset or having a bad day. You've had days where you have been upset about something. The best thing to do for someone in that position is to listen to them talk about it. As they get it out of their system, they'll feel better, and you will, too.

10. **Donate Your Time:** Many places could use some help, whether it be a shelter for families in need or an elderly program that helps people in your neighborhood stay safe and happy.

11. **Do Someone a Favor:** When someone is stressed or having a bad day, they don't always want to talk about it. Sometimes, the best thing you can do is help them out with something else. If you are good at something (like cooking or cleaning), offer to do that for them even if they don't ask for it.

12. **Hold the Door for Someone:** It's a small gesture, but holding the door open for people who are behind you is helpful. It shows others that you are a kind person and that you care about people. Of course, if you're feeling particularly benevolent, you can offer to walk someone's dog or help someone with their groceries.

13. **Say Sorry:** No one likes to be hurt, even by accident. If you have hurt someone, always say sorry. They will appreciate your apology, and so will everyone else who witnesses your kindness.

14. **Donate:** When you have extra toys or clothes, why not donate them to someone who needs them more than you do? You'll be doing a good thing for someone and making space for more items.

15. **Donate Blood:** At the age of 17, you are eligible to donate blood. This huge sacrifice can save another person's life and is completely safe.

16. **Offer Words of Encouragement:** Everyone needs a little encouragement sometimes. Give it to them by telling them how great they are doing or by saying you're proud of them. Their self-confidence will go up, and they'll be all the more motivated to continue succeeding.

17. **Do Chores Without Being Asked:** If you see that your sister or brother has been living in a messy room or something around the house that needs tidying up, don't wait to be asked to do it. Instead, offer to help out.

18. **Be a buddy to a new student:** If you come across a new student at your school, try to be friendly and helpful by offering to show them around. Introduce them to other students and involve

them in group activities. Your kindness can help them feel more comfortable and less nervous.

19. **Start a kindness club:** Form a club at your school dedicated to spreading kindness. Brainstorm ideas together, plan activities like fundraisers for charities, or organize kindness-themed events to get others to join in and spread kindness even further.

20. **Make "Kindness Rocks":** Find smooth stones or rocks and decorate them with brightly colored paints or markers. Write positive messages or draw happy pictures on them. Then, place the rocks in public spaces like parks or playgrounds for others to discover. You never know whose face you'll put a smile on.

You don't have to go out and start a huge project to help others. It really doesn't take much to give back to your community. Instead, be creative in your random acts of kindness, and you'll be surprised at how good you can make other people feel.

CROSSWORDS PUZZLES

Across

2. What spreads rapidly on the internet?
4. What are polite ways of behaving?
7. How do you treat others with admiration?
10. What is polite behavior called?
12. What is fair behavior in sports called?
13. What is the feeling of being thankful?
14. Not being successful in a game?

Down

1. What is being friendly and considerate?
3. What is the bond between caring people?
5. What is focusing on something or someone?
6. Opposite of losing in a game?
8. Polite word for a request?
9. What is feeling sure of yourself?
11. Who intentionally upsets others online?

Conclusion

Having good manners means showing respect for others and their unique qualities. Being sociable and polite makes you an amazing person! Being kind makes the world a better place, makes those around you happy, and makes you likable. You can give the gift of kindness to others, which will make them feel great about themselves and about you.

Now that you have these new skills in your toolbox, it's time to put them to good use. Use them when interacting with people in social situations, with friends and family, at school, and in everyday life. Remember that good manners are not just about following rules but also about genuinely caring for others and creating a positive atmosphere wherever you go. By being respectful and kind and saying please and thank you, you will earn respect and admiration from those around you and become a role model for others to follow. Imagine a world where everyone treated each other with respect. It would be a much brighter and happier place to live. So, go ahead and spread the magic of good manners, and watch as it transforms your relationships and the world around you.

Check out another book in the series

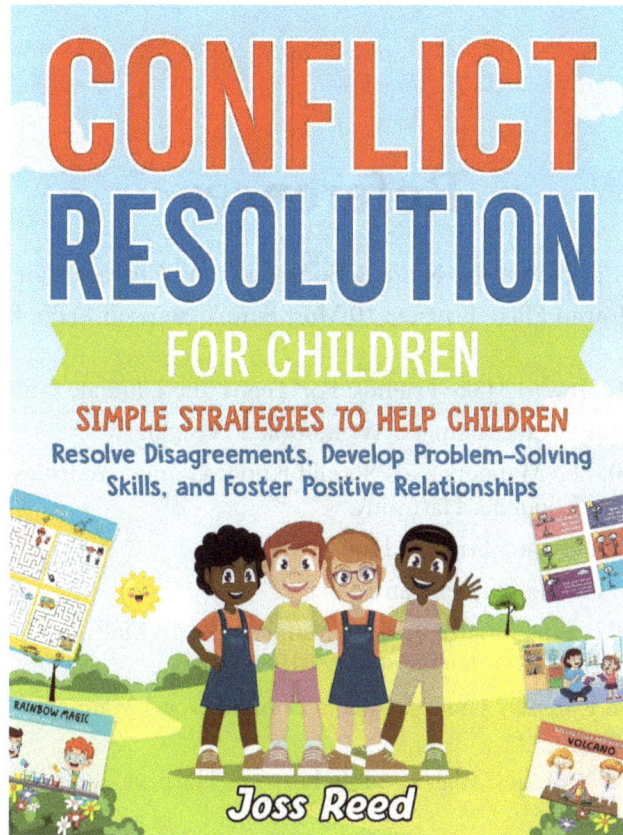

References

Townsend, E. (2020, August 12). How to Be Kind: A Book on Good Character for Young Readers.

Johnson, A. (2015, May 5). How to Make Friends: 10 Most Simple Steps to Make Friends for Life - and How to Retain Them!

Love, J. (2014, November 24). How to Make Friends: For Teens (the Ultimate Guide for Teens).

Harding, L. (2020, July 23). Mind Your Manners: Workbook 2 (Vol. 2).

Eberly, S. (2011, November 8). 365 Manners Kids Should Know: Games, Activities, and Other Fun Ways to Help Children and Teens Learn Etiquette. Harmony.

Heos, B. (2015, August 1). Manners at a Friend's House.

Cornwall, P. (2010, August 1). Online Etiquette and Safety.

Senning, C. P., & Post, P. (2007, September 25). Teen Manners: From Malls to Meals to Messaging and Beyond. HarperTeen. https://doi.org/10.1604/9780060881986

Santorum, K. (2003, April 30). Everyday Graces: Child's Book of Good Manners. https://doi.org/10.1604/9781932236095

Rosenthal, A. K. (2006, May 2). Cookies: Bite-Size Life Lessons. HarperCollins. https://doi.org/10.1604/9780060580810